The Secret World of
Spies

Meredith Costain

ETA Cuisenaire

Cuisenaire
800-445-5985   www.etacuisenaire.com

The Secret World of Spies

ISBN 978-0-7406-1565-8
ETA 303091

ETA/Cuisenaire • Vernon Hills, IL 60061-1862
800-445-5985 • www.etacuisenaire.com

Text © 2001 Meredith Costain
Illustrations © 2001 Lisa Coutts
Designer: Caroline Laird
Acknowledgments: Cover, 28, Getty Images; 4, 12, 29, Australian Picture
Library/Corbis; 20, Photo © Powerhouse Museum, Sydney, 1994 (Photographer:
Jane Townsend); 30, Space Imaging PR/Genesis.

Printed in China (SWTC/04)

10 11 12   10 9 8 7 6 5 4

Contents

What Is a **Spy?**

Spies collect and deliver secret information. They enter enemy territory to gather valuable facts and secrets. The spy profession is older and more difficult than you may realize. From the beginnings of history, spies have come up with amazing ways to complete their missions.

We often picture a spy as a shadowy figure wearing a trench coat, dark glasses, and a hat — or as a slick character equipped with amazing high-tech gadgets.

Ancient **Spies**

Spying began thousands of years ago! Kings and rulers paid spies to sneak into the camps of their enemies. The spies counted the number of warriors there, or listened while the enemy discussed plans for attack. If the spies were successful, they became heroes and received big rewards. If they failed – and were caught – they were executed.

Can you find the spy? Someone is watching these warriors.

One of the earliest known cases of spying occurred in ancient Egypt. Archaeologists have found a clay tablet from the year 1370 B.C. The tablet contains an order from an ancient Syrian leader instructing an official to spy on the Queen of Egypt.

Spying was a highly-valued skill in ancient China. A famous warrior by the name of Sun Tzu (say *soo*) wrote a book called *The Art of War*. In it, he describes the importance of spying in times of war. Sun Tzu said that "if you know the enemy and know yourself, you need not fear a hundred battles."

Working
Undercover

Spying is dangerous work. Spying missions are usually top secret and sometimes involve working "undercover." With a disguise, spies can protect their true identity and hide their secret activities from the enemy.

Is this window washer really an undercover spy?

Dressed to Impress

One clever spy named Chevalier D'Eon (say *sha-VA-le-ay d-oh*) worked for King Louis XV of France in 1755. Disguised as a noblewoman, he carried a letter from the King to the Russian Empress. The Russian Court was very suspicious of the French at this time. D'Eon would not have been able to meet with the Empress as a Frenchman.

Dressed as a lady, Chevalier D'Eon was able to befriend the Empress. He was even made her maid of honor!

Spy Baby

The youngest spy in the history of spying was a spy named Richeberg (say *reesh-bear*) from France. He was unusually small for his age and was able to go undercover as a child during the French Revolution.

Richeberg carried secret documents that were hidden in his clothes in and out of Paris.

Butterfly Secrets

During the Boer War in South Africa, British spy Lord Baden-Powell found an inventive way to carry out his spy work. Baden-Powell pretended to be an innocent butterfly collector drawing rare butterflies.

Baden-Powell's drawings of butterflies actually contained secret diagrams of enemy defenses!

Double Trouble

A special kind of undercover spy is a double agent. These spies pretend they are working for one spying organization when they are really working for another. Colonel Penkovsky (say *pen-KOV-ski*) was a spy working for the Russian Military Intelligence in the 1960s. The Russians didn't know that he was a double agent in disguise!

Penkovsky photographed thousands of top secret Russian documents and delivered the film to the British and American governments.

Top Secret
Delivery

Throughout history, there are tales of spies who have come up with clever ways to hide and pass on important secrets. Paul Bernard, a French mapmaker, had this down to a fine art. His writing was so small, he was able to hide a 1600-word report under a stamp on a postcard!

A Close Shave

In 500 B.C., Histiaeus (say *his-TAY-oose*), the ruler of Miletus, found an unusual way to get a message to his loyal friend Aristagaros (say *ar-is-TAG-a-rus*), who was being held by enemy guards. Histiaeus shaved the head of his most trusted slave, and wrote the message on his scalp.

After the hair had grown back, the slave was sent to ask Aristagaros to "shave his head, then look carefully at it."

A Load of Old Hay

During the Civil War in America, there was a rich Union spy named Elizabeth Van Lew. She kept her horse in her hay-filled upstairs library. Van Lew used the horse to deliver messages to other Union spies at night.

The horse was so quiet, an enemy officer who was boarding at the house never knew it was there.

Hidden Secrets

Spies have concealed many important documents
and plans as they passed through enemy lines.
Betty Duvall was a Confederate agent in the
Civil War. She carried coded messages in her
long black hair. Louise de Bettignes (say *be-tin-
yay*) was a French spy in World War I. She hid a
tiny map in the frame of a pair of glasses.

Louise de Bettignes also hid messages inside balls of
knitting yarn.

Coded
Messages

Spies often need to deliver secret messages and information to each other. They use codes to make sure the messages don't fall into the wrong hands. A code is a group of words, letters, or symbols that have been given a secret meaning.

A simple sentence in a letter, such as "the flowers are now in bloom," may really mean "we need to arrange a meeting."

Staff Secrets

One of the earliest methods used to disguise a message involved a wooden staff.

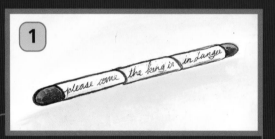

1

2

The sender would wrap a piece of paper around a staff and write a message on it.

The sender would then unwind the paper.

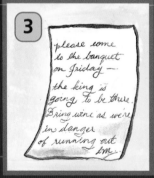

3

4

The sender would fill in the spaces in the message with other words. This would hide the real message.

To read the message, the receiver would have to wrap the paper around another wooden staff of the same size.

The Caesar Cipher

In ancient Rome, Julius Caesar (say *SEE-zer*) invented a simple way to conceal secret information from his enemies. This became known as the "Caesar Cipher." Caesar rearranged the alphabet so that each letter was moved three places: A became D, B became E, C became F, and so on.

Alphabet

A B C D E F G H I J K L M N O P Q R S T U V W X Y Z

D E F G H I J K L M N O P Q R S T U V W X Y Z A B C

Cipher

Using this cipher, the word SECRET would be written VHFUHW.

The Enigma Machine

Just before World War II, German scientists invented a special coding machine called the Enigma. The machine looked kind of like a typewriter. It was able to convert messages into a special code. The only way to decode the message was by using another Enigma machine.

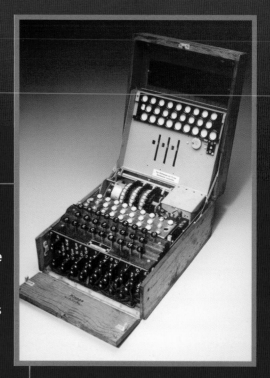

The British made a copy of the Enigma. Then they were able to decode many of Germany's messages during the war.

He Blew It!

The award for the silliest spy goes to the man who was hired to blow up the coding machine inside a German embassy. He was asked to blow up the most complicated-looking machine he could find. Unfortunately, he didn't know very much about modern machinery.

The spy snuck past the guards and exploded a machine. The next day, however, the Germans were still sending out coded messages. The daredevil had blown up the electric coffee maker!

Backward Words

Write each word in your message backward.

Meet me at the old pier.
becomes
Teem em ta eht dlo reip.

Backward Sentences

Write the whole sentence backward.

Meet me at the old pier.
becomes
Reip dlo eht ta em teem.

Secret Messages

Extra First Letters

Place an extra letter in front of each word in your message. To break the code, your partner needs to cross out the first letter of each word.

Meet me at the old pier.
becomes
Smeet ome cat othe bold spier.

Decode this message.

SWELL EDONE. OYOU
SHAVE TCRACKED ITHE
ACODE.

Answer on page 31.

23

Alphabet Code

Use the alphabet to help write your message in code. First write down your message. Use capital letters. Spread out the letters.

M E E T   M E   A T   M I D N I G H T.

Then write the letter of the alphabet that comes after each of the letters in your message. Write underneath each letter.

M E E T   M E   A T   M I D N I G H T.
N F F U   N F   B U   N J E O J H I U.

Now write your coded message on a new piece of paper.

N F F U   N F   B U   N J E O J H I U.

To decode the message, the receiver needs to write down the letter of the alphabet that comes before each of the letters in the message.

Decode this message.

T Q J F T   V T F   D P E F T
U P   L F F Q   U I F J S   N F T T B H F T
U P Q   T F D S F U

Answer on page 31.

Invisible Writing

Send your partner a coded message using invisible ink.

You will need the following:

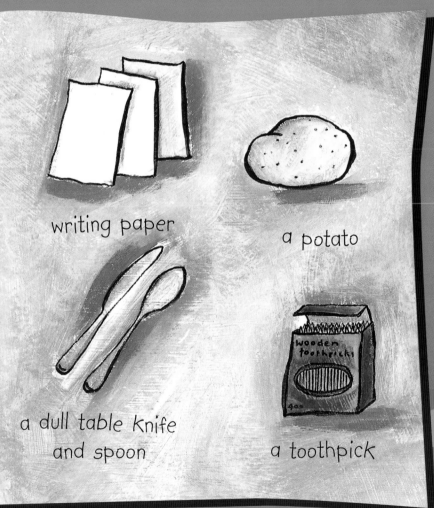

writing paper

a potato

a dull table knife
and spoon

a toothpick

What to Do

1 Cut the top and bottom off the potato so that you have flat surfaces to work with. Save the pieces.

2 Scoop a hole in the potato with a spoon.

3 Scrape juice from the pieces into the hole.

4 Dip the toothpick into the juice. Use the potato juice to write a message on the paper.

5 Allow the paper to dry. Your message will now be invisible!

6 Ask your partner to put the paper in the sun. The message will reappear!

Modern **Spies**

Spies today can live dangerous lives. Their job is still to track down secret information and pass it on to their employers, without being caught! There are now entire government departments devoted to spy work. Also, large private companies might hire people to spy on their competitors.

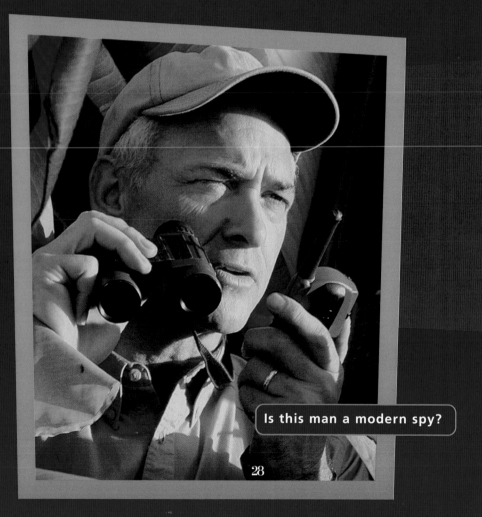

Is this man a modern spy?

Modern technology has changed the world of spying. It is possible for spies to listen in on telephone conversations or catch your every move on video cameras. There are also spies who have become very skilled at stealing information from other people's computers.

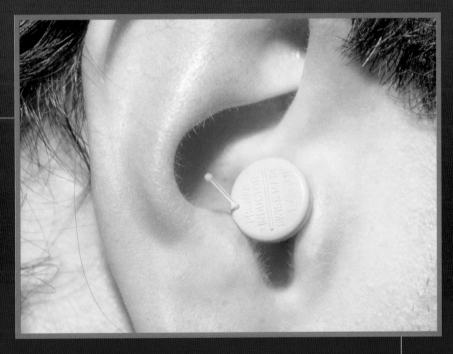

Would you have noticed this? It is a tiny ear microphone.

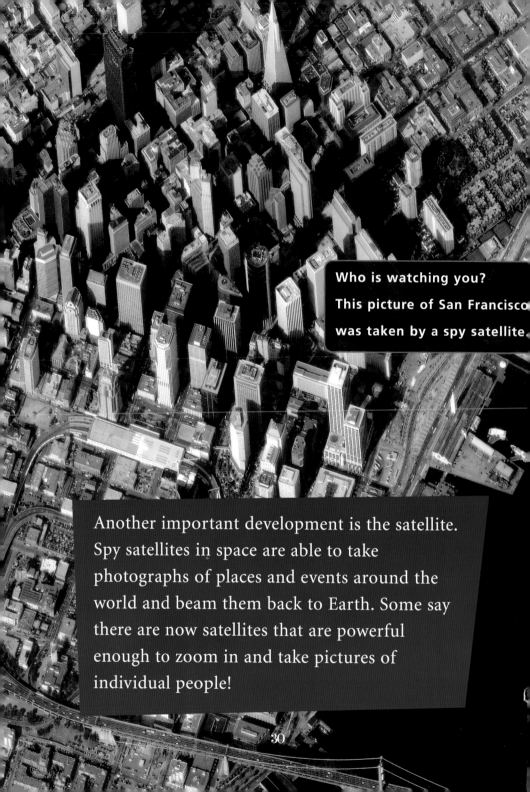

Who is watching you?
This picture of San Francisco
was taken by a spy satellite.

Another important development is the satellite.
Spy satellites in space are able to take
photographs of places and events around the
world and beam them back to Earth. Some say
there are now satellites that are powerful
enough to zoom in and take pictures of
individual people!

Glossary

archaeologist	a person who studies the remains of an ancient culture
cipher	a kind of code
competitor	a business rival
identity	who a person is
mission	an important job that a person is sent to do
noblewoman	a woman of high social rank
satellite	a spacecraft that moves around a planet
territory	an area of land that belongs to a country or person
warrior	a person who fights in a battle

Secret message on page 23:
Well done. You have cracked the code.
Secret message on page 25:
Spies use codes to keep their messages top secret.

Index